13043 ⅓2

STEAM SPECIALS

British Rail's Return to Steam

Roger Siviter

With special feature by Bernard Staite

DAVID & CHARLES
Newton Abbot   London   North Pomfret (Vt)

Class 9F 2–10–0 No 92203 *Black Prince* makes a fine
sight as it steams out of Westbury with a special bound for
the Open Day at Eastleigh Works on 20 April 1975.

CONTENTS

British Library Cataloguing in Publication Data

Siviter, Roger
  Steam specials.
1. Locomotives – Great Britain – History
  – 20th century
  I. Title
  385'.361'0941   TJ603.4.G7

  ISBN 0 7153 8126 1

© Roger Siviter 1981

Photoset by
Northern Phototypesetting Co
Bolton
Printed in Great Britain
by Biddles Ltd Guildford
for David & Charles (Publishers) Limited
Brunel House Newton Abbot Devon

Published in the United States of America
by David & Charles Inc
North Pomfret Vermont 05053 USA

INTRODUCTION

11 August 1968. That date will go down in history as the end of main line steam on British Railways. At the time and indeed for the next three years it seemed to enthusiasts that apart from the odd trip by *Flying Scotsman*, which had a special contract with BR, we should never see steam again on the main line. There was steam operation on the growing number of privately preserved branch railways but it was not the same. In any case the larger express locomotives were barred from most of these branches by weight and clearances. But thanks to the efforts of a group of enthusiasts, and Bulmers of Hereford, BR relented. On 2 October, 1971 *King George V*, on loan to Bulmers, steamed out of Hereford station for what was to be the first of very many steam specials that have been run over the last ten years.

At first these trips were confined to a few routes and a small number of locomotives. As time has gone by more and more routes have been approved for use by steam and now a fairly large fleet of steam locomotives, many privately owned, operate on these journeys into the past. In the light of experience some routes have since been taken off the list.

The general map of lines approved for steam opposite is supplemented by more detailed maps of what I consider to be the busiest steam routes, namely Newport–Chester, Leeds–Carlisle, Skipton–Carnforth–Sellafield and the York area, and gradient profiles of Newport–Chester and Skipton–Carlisle lines.

Some years have seen more special trains than others, notable being 1975 and 1980, the years of the Shildon and Rainhill 150th anniversary celebrations. These events brought the movement of locomotives from many parts of the country to the respective events and resulted in several fascinating workings. Who would ever have thought of seeing *Maude*, a North British 0–6–0, climbing over Ais Gill, or a Great Western Manor at York station?

I have tried to show in the pictorial section of the book as large a cross section of specials as possible, but obviously certain routes have been used more than others. The same applies to the locomotives. I suppose *Flying Scotsman* and *King George V* to name two, have been used on more runs than many other engines but I have tried to show the unusual as well as what one might term the expected.

Remember, though, that steam operation is a business and needs an immense amount of work behind the scenes by the promoters to ensure smooth operation and adequate financial return to BR which clearly cannot run steam trips at a loss. To fit in steam trains on an otherwise all-diesel and electric state-run system is no mean feat. But it can have commercial attractions as BR has found with its regular steam excursions from Carnforth and the York Circular. The special feature in this book by Bernard Staite of the Steam Locomotive Operators Association describes the trials, tribulations and humorous side of running steam specials. We must not forget also the many volunteers who through their efforts enable so many of us to enjoy steam on the main line and of course the many BR staff involved in timing offices, on the trains and elsewhere.

Finally my thanks go to Joan Wappett for the typing and my wife Christina for all the help she has given me in the preparation of this book.

Roger Siviter

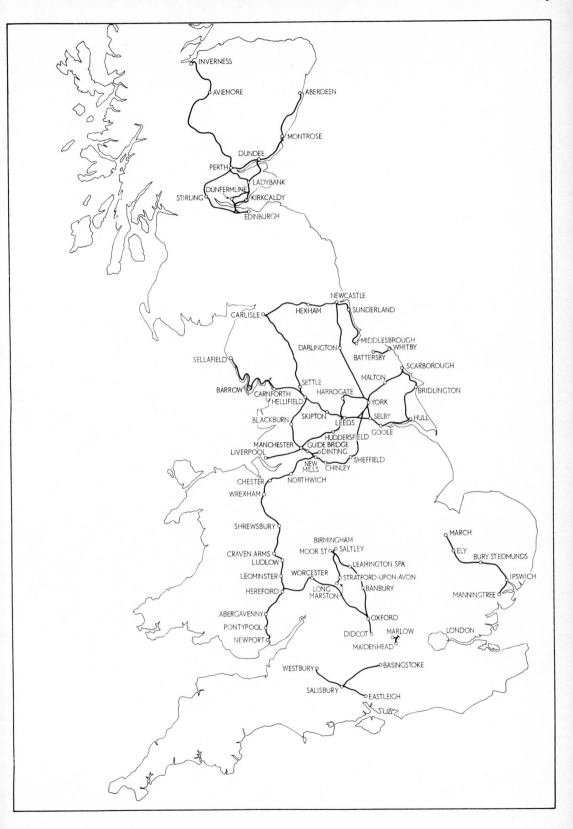

6

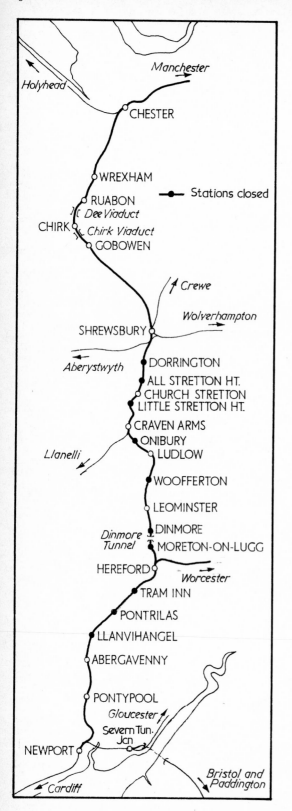

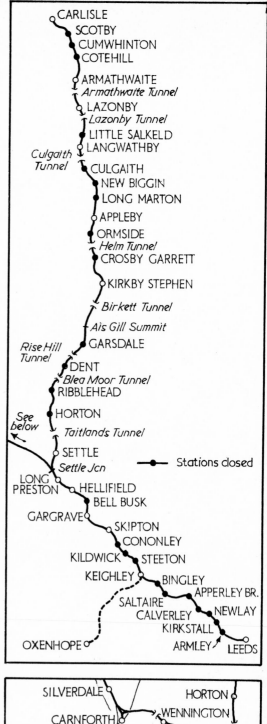

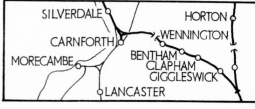

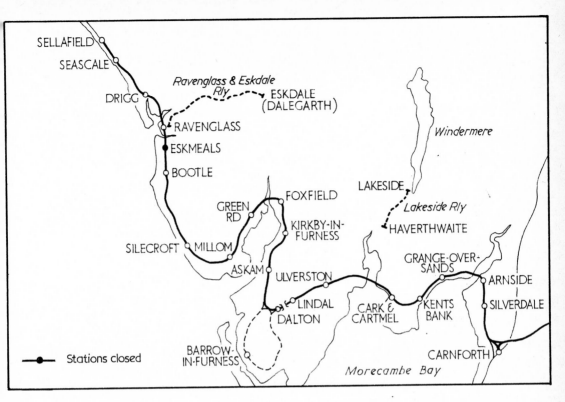

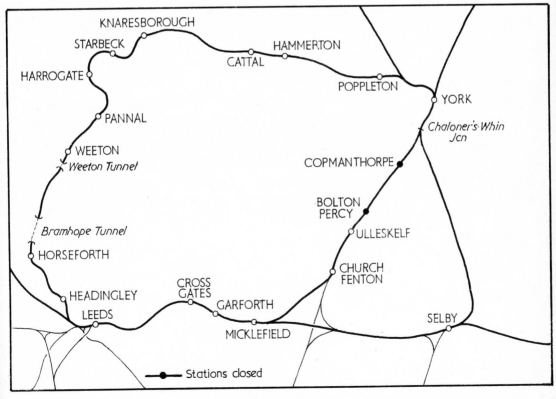

TEN GLORIOUS YEARS OF STEAM

Bernard Staite (Secretary, Steam Locomotive Operators Association).

RETURN TO STEAM. What problems and difficulties those three words meant at the end of the 1960s and the start of the 1970s, for the dedicated band of enthusiasts and individuals who had acquired one of the out-moded, and definitely out-of-fashion, steam locomotives from BR, when our railways decided to concentrate on diesel and electric traction to the total exclusion of steam from August 1968. There was no way the modern Inter-City network, with its supporting secondary services, would see or hear again one of the majestic giants, which had served us so well for more than 140 years. Indeed there was an official Ban on Steam! The powers at the BRB at that time would not budge. Steam was contrary to the image which they wanted for the new BR and that was that — or was it? Bulmer's Cider, which as a company had acquired the flagship of the former GWR, No. 6000 *King George V*, on loan from Swindon Corporation, had restored it to full working order in the hope that one day it might head the Bulmer's Cider train of restored Pullman cars over British Rail metals. Peter Prior, the then managing director, set out to achieve this particular aim.

During the summer of 1970, Paul Barnes and a production unit were filming *KGV*, as 6000 is affectionately known, on behalf of the National Coal Board as a tribute by the Board to the Age of Steam. Certainly the NCB had lost possibly its biggest ever customer two years earlier, but it was still prepared to acknowledge the impact made by steam locomotives and as such, and unknown at the time, this particular film *6000, King George V* was to play a major part some nine months later in helping to pave the way for the long awaited return to steam. Incidentally, it was ironic that Paul Barnes' superb work had also paid tribute to the end of steam on BR with his unforgettable film *Black 5*. This was filmed almost entirely at

Carnforth, now the home of Steamtown and probably the centre most involved with current steam operation on BR. The Barnes' *KGV* production was chosen as the supporting feature for the 1971 Royal Command Film Performance and, to his eternal credit, Peter Prior saw to it that he and senior representatives from British Rail were in attendance to see 'his' engine on the big screen. The actual command film was *Love Story* and certainly this had some bearing on the evening, for the title describes what the steam locomotive meant to those dedicated to seeing it again in full cry out on BR at the head of a train. Peter Prior's persuasive powers had probably never been better that night and in the subsequent weeks, for, some three months later, the BRB, from its Marylebone headquarters, gave the go-ahead for 6000 to make an experimental run on British Rail in the Autumn, with the Bulmer's Cider train, to examine the problems associated with working the occasional steam-hauled excursion. The ban had been breached and lifted, albeit for a trial period!

The Western Region board room at Paddington was where it all started. Detailed outline arrangements were made by the meeting which lasted virtually all day. Problems and objections were raised but all along there was the underlying knowledge that BR was to see steam again with a passenger train. And thus it was that 6000, in all its glory, left Hereford on a foggy 2 October, 1971, at the start of a week's tour and exhibition of the Bulmer's Cider train. The operation of the trial has been extremely well chronicled elsewhere; suffice it to say that the experiment was a resounding success, and that agreement was reached with British Rail for a limited number of steam-hauled excursions in the future. We had returned to steam, in the main through the tireless efforts of Peter Prior. Ten years on, it is with pleasure and gratitude that his name is recorded here. Let none of us forget his contribution!

Also in that ten years, many hundreds of tons of coal and thousands upon thousands of gallons of water have made steam on BR. These ten years have brought countless pleasure and enjoyment to thousands who have been thrilled by the sights, sounds and, indeed, smells of the main line

Previous page: Pictured south of York near Copmanthorpe on 10 May 1980, is LMS Stanier 4–6–2 No 46229 *Duchess of Hamilton* with The Limited Edition York circular train. This run heralded the return of No 46229 to main line working.

locomotive, out where it was meant to be at the head of a train, in steam and running at speed. But equally it is only there through the continuing efforts, largely unpaid, of the steam enthusiasts or devotees − call us what you will − and of course, the much appreciated co-operation and goodwill of British Rail itself at all levels.

Certainly in the ten years that have elapsed since *KGV's* October venture in 1971, BR's attitude has changed out of all recognition, so much so that BR itself entered the steam market in 1978 with its highly successful Cumbrian Coast Express. This was steam-hauled from Carnforth to Sellafield and return, with locomotives being prepared and disposed of at Carnforth by volunteer support crews. The initiative for BR's first step into the steam market stemmed from the London Midland Region. It is to be applauded for its continuing and active support of such services, recognising of course that while it is acknowledged that steam has a part to play in earning revenue, such revenue in this day and age, with ever increasing costs, can only be marginal both to British Rail and the locomotive operators. Definitely such revenue can only be looked at from the leisure market point of view, as in no way can we, or indeed should we, expect British Rail even to consider regular commercial steam operation; as my chairman in SLOA often says, 'we are really in partnership with BR in show business!'

So where have we got to? What have we done? What of the future? How do we put on the steam specials? During the period 1972 to 1975 individual locomotive owners/operators to a very large degree did their own thing; they ran or let their locomotives haul a variety of trains over the approved steam routes, which British Rail had drawn up, without any real co-ordination. Most of the steam-hauled excursions ran but others failed through lack of support. Each of the operators made individual approaches to British Rail, which in turn spent a disproportionate amount of time and effort in progressing and organising the special trains. Much of the income generated − and let us be clear right from the start, no one with a main line locomotive is going to cover maintenance costs, let alone make a profit, from operating on British Rail − went to outside parties rather than the main line locomotives. So all in all, the movement was crying out for organisation. To this end, the Steam Locomotive Operators' Association (SLOA − pun intended!) was formed. The only criteria for membership is that the

operator or individual must have responsibility for a registered main line locomotive. Before any locomotive can operate a passenger train on BR metals, it has to be registered by BR, following − quite rightly − stringent examinations by BR's chief mechanical engineer's inspectorate, both mechanically and particularly from the boiler point of view. Those which have passed these examinations, have achieved, if you like, the ultimate, and believe me it is not easy or cheap! We have the safest railway system in the world and no exceptions are or indeed can be made for the occasional canter by a steam locomotive.

British Rail welcomed the formation of SLOA as it meant that BR now only dealt with one organisation, which in turn prepared a co-ordinated programme of steam trains for its consideration. As time has progressed, so the relationship between BR and the Association has gone from strength to strength, with all aspects of steam operation dealt with totally between the Association and British Rail. To illustrate this, BR representatives regularly attend and play an active part in SLOA meetings and, once a year, an Annual Policy Review meeting is convened between BR and SLOA to discuss all aspects of policy, for example, approval of and consideration of new steam running routes, attitudes towards boiler regulations, pricing, etc. In all, we have come a million miles since 1970, having entered into a virtual partnership with BR for main line steam operation.

Steam running on British Rail is controlled by the Steam Policy Document prepared by the BRB in conjunction with the regions, and nowadays discussed with SLOA prior to finalisation, and also issued on a three-yearly or five-yearly basis as opposed to annually in the earlier years. BR was quick to agree with SLOA's request for this type of policy duration in the light of costly boiler repairs, lifting etc. Currently, to re-tube a locomotive we are talking of £10,000 to £20,000. If the Steam Policy were not to continue in the following year, what a costly and needless exercise this would be! The Policy Document is reviewed as indicated earlier on an annual basis with the present Policy going forward to the end of 1985 and hopefully the chance of at-least a three-year renewal thereafter.

SLOA members discuss and agree a programme of steam tours amongst themselves, in line with the Policy Document, for submission to British Rail for approval. This is generally for a session, for example, Spring (1 April to 31 May) or

Autumn (15 September to 31 December). Incidentally, a gentlemen's agreement exists with British Rail whereby BR sponsors its own trains in the summer session, generally mid-week, as coaching stock resources are at a premium over weekends, as indeed they are at the shoulders of the Spring and Autumn sessions. Once agreement is given by British Rail, and coaching stock allocated, the BR price is drawn up from previously agreed rates per seat. Charges are added by the locomotive operator for the steam traction, direct costs, coal, water, lubricants, etc, together with a financial contribution for the locomotive's long term maintenance. Insurance for both public liability (BR requires £2 million cover) and accident are included in the budget and to these items are added the cost of promotion and marketing, ie advertising, booking forms, and publicity, etc. Then the overall budget cost for the operation is drawn up. From the number of seats available, fares are calculated and the 'Show gets on the road' with SLOA corporate advertising, a SLOA policy to pull in the enquiries and the eventual bookings. The policy of the Association nowadays is that only the locomotive operator working the train can in fact market it, otherwise SLOA's own marketing division takes over. This is simply to ensure that any excess revenue generated is ploughed back into the main line movement and in particular the maintenance of the locomotives. However, block bookings, which attract discounts, are always welcome (forgive the plug!) and indeed some trains are entirely block booked by a society for example.

The movement is composed of virtually two departments for train operation, the commercial which looks after all promotion, marketing and on-train arrangements, and the largely unsung but vital locomotive department which struggles and toils long into the night and, indeed, early hours of the morning to have the engine in top class condition, first for the British Rail inspection, because nothing leaves the depot without an inspection, and then for the paying supporters on the train. Both departments will be doing their utmost to ensure that everything will be alright on the day. At the end of it, the passenger will go home satisfied with the product, because if not, and he does not come again, it will be increasingly difficult to fill the trains. It is perhaps difficult, especially when contributing to a photographic album, to get this message across to the lineside photographer. But remember photographers have

a responsibility to contribute and, without the paying passengers, there would be nothing to capture on film. In saying this, many of the linesiders do contribute, some quite handsomely, and to all of them we offer our grateful thanks.

TEN MORE YEARS?
Now, to the future. This is dependent on three things and not necessarily in this order. First money and more money; locomotives are extremely expensive items to maintain for the main line. Second, the continued goodwill and availability of British Rail footplatemen and technical inspectors; remember regular steam finished on British Rail over 12 years ago. You try shovelling five or six tons of coal on a moving work surface once or twice a year! Third, the desire of the general public to spend whatever excess money they have, on a day out with a difference. All of us in SLOA will do our utmost to ensure that the locomotives are available to haul the trains, given the continued excellent support from British Rail at all levels and the fare-paying passengers.

As far as the type of operation is concerned, and given a crystal ball, I believe we shall see more of the highly successful Cumbrian Mountain Express and Welsh Marches Express type of package operation. British Rail is certainly very much in favour of this concept as obviously once set up, it virtually becomes a timetable service with no more real managerial and administrative effort after the first train for anything up to a dozen or more. Contrary to previous policy requirements, locomotives are permitted to transfer between depots to work these services, thereby ensuring that all of the locomotives get the opportunity to share in the work. Who knows, we may yet see Ais Gill looking like Wembley on Cup Final Day, when and if we can get a 'copper capped' machine up to the north and over the mountains. We shall see an increased involvement by British Rail with its own sponsored operations, as both the Eastern and Scottish Regions intend joining the pioneering LMR with their own services in 1981, traction being supplied by appropriate SLOA members. We may see a contraction in some of the routes from 1983 onwards because of revised passenger traffic flows and the availability of manpower, but bear in mind over a thousand miles of line is now approved for steam.

The question of new locomotives is difficult. We have nearly 40 on the registered (approved) list

Return to Steam. *King George V* steams slowly through the mist out of Hereford station on 2 October 1971, the first main line steam trip after the ban was lifted, from Hereford to Tyseley.

now. Should we go on adding ad infinitum, thereby reducing everyone's earning potential, to keep the current locomotives in tip-top condition, or do we say 'enough is enough' and ensure a top class more limited fleet into the 1990s? Given the continuing support for steam we have at present this is an extremely difficult and emotive question. People often ask what are we going to do about rolling stock. Having mentioned a possible continuation beyond 1985, from the annual reviews with BR it is clear that stock will be available for steam haulage, certainly to the end of the 1980s and into the early 1990s. The future is there still for all of us to grasp, to enjoy the sight and sounds of the giants of steam that we seemed to have lost for ever, just over ten years ago.

Returning to the events of 1971 and the film *Love Story*, certainly our return to steam is like such a story, for the last ten years have had their moments of sadness as well as joy, though mainly the latter. Steam locomotives have been likened by many to being alive; most definitely they are temperamental, just like humans. Witness the occasional failure we have had out on the road and the odd refusal to climb a bank, and then contrast the exhilarating runs we have had. All this shows just why the steam locomotive has and will continue to have that special place in our affections.

We have had moments of sadness with our supporters too. Indeed all of us in SLOA can recount our own stories. Let me dwell on just two with *KGV*. A 12 year old blind boy, thrilling to the sound of 6000 on its way to Newport, couldn't visualise anything at all about a steam locomotive; but when told that 6000 carried a bell just like his local church bells, he was lifted on to the buffer beam at Newport and rang the bell for himself, describing the moment – and remember he could not see and had never seen a steam locomotive – as the greatest thing in his young life. There was sadness for the boy but also joy to experience the pleasure that he had got just from the sounds of that day. The second was a 30 year old, whose only ambition was to stand on the footplate of 6000 which he had never done before; as he did so, he thanked us and begged us to continue running on the main line as long as we could. A fortnight later he passed away from cancer but a letter from his wife brought testament to the thrill he had had from being on the footplate. It was such a small thing. Those of us who enjoy good health and have the ability to participate have a duty therefore to keep steaming. Let us hope we can, and we shall certainly try. Thankfully joy with steam is a commodity that far outweighs the sadness. We have certainly generated considerable joy in running out on the main line again with steam traction. Just travel on the annual Santa Steam Special and see the faces of the younger generation, our future supporters, to believe it; talk to the senior citizens who travel with us and walk through a train when steam is at the head, and you will see joy.

Inevitably in the ten years since the return to steam there have been some humorous events. I could relate many but as I am 'watching the road' at the moment, they will have to wait for another day. Nevertheless, with Rocket 150 still very much in mind and as the main line fraternity played such an extremely large part in providing the steam locomotives, I can recount two incidents at Bold, that dusty outpost which was to be our shed for the event. The first concerns the technical staff of BR's Advanced Passenger Train who were somewhat upset and could not understand why we made smoke with our engines as it was dirtying the APT; could we perhaps not use as much coal! Perhaps they did not realise that their APT also makes smoke, albeit from a power station. Secondly, we had, quite inadvertently, the greatest tug or war I have ever seen. I was acting as shunter during the three days at Bold and on the Saturday evening had 35028, 5690, 6201 and 46229 coupled together in that order. I signalled for the four locomotives to go forward with the Duchess leading, but 35028's crew misread me (or so they said) and tried to set back, smoke, steam, noise – I had never seen or heard anything like it! Contrary to all expectations, the Bullied machine not only held its ground but actually, or so it is alleged, moved a foot or two against the tide! Needless to say, the air was blue and the 'clanker's' footplate crew's faces were red; another story had been born to go into the memory book and to be discussed over the pints when the fires were banked. Underneath it all, there is an outstanding fellowship amongst those of us who are privileged to carry the main line torch.

Before shutting the regulator and going on shed, may I pay tribute to the work of Roger Siviter, a quiet unassuming man but an artist with a camera, who has recorded for posterity in the following pages the sight of main line steam in the 1970s, a sight that we thought we might never see again. Let me ask Roger and the reader if they would give and accept the pictures as dedications to the professional railwaymen at all levels, in particular the footplatemen, together with their amateur cousins, who keep the locomotives running and sell the trains. Their joint efforts and co-operation have ensured enjoyment for thousands, and kept a little of the heritage of the country where the railway was born alive and well, to show our children, and, who knows, their children, something of what main line steam was and is all about. Here's to 1991!

SLOA members 1981
A4 Locomotive Society
Dinting Railway Centre
Steamtown Carnforth
Great Western Society (GWS)

Humberside Locomotive Preservation Group (HLPG)
Severn Valley Railway (SVR)
Leander Locomotive
Princess Elizabeth Locomotive Society (PELS)
National Railway Museum (NRM)
Birmingham Railway Museum (BRM)
6000 Locomotive Association (6000 LA)
North Eastern Locomotive Preservation Group (NELPG)
13809 Group
Merchant Navy Locomotive Preservation Society (MNLPS)
Scottish Railway Preservation Society (SRPS)
J B Cameron
Friends of the National Railway Museum (FNRM)

Below: Gradient profile, Leeds–Carlisle.

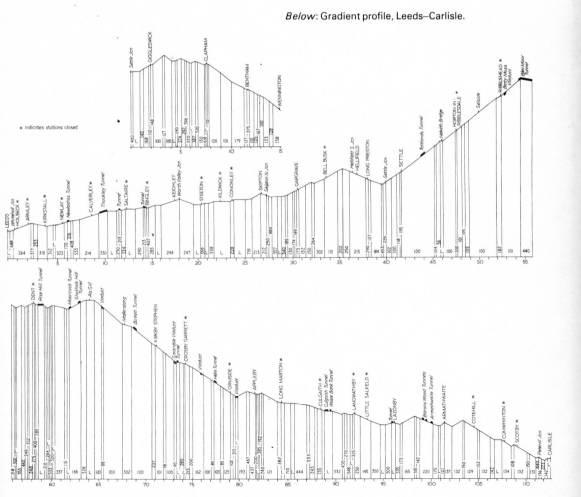

16

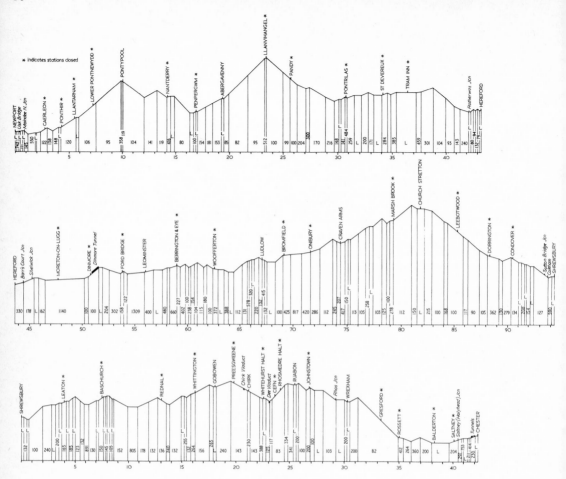

Gradient profile, Newport, Hereford, Shrewsbury, Chester.

Speeding south out of Green Houses tunnel, Culgaith, on the Carlisle–Settle line, is Jubilee 4–6–0 No 5690 *Leander* on 26 April 1980.

Top left: 22 September 1979 saw No 4930 *Hagley Hall* and LMS Class 5 4–6–0 No 5000 hauling the Inter City between Hereford and Chester and return. The pair are seen on the outward journey just north of Church Stretton. This train was organised by the Severn Valley Railway.

Left: No 7808 *Cookham Manor* and 6998 *Burton Agnes Hall* climb Hatton Bank on 19 October 1974, with a Great Western Society special from Didcot to Tyseley via Stratford-on-Avon formed of a splendid array of preserved GWR coaches.

Above: No 5690 *Leander* climbs up to Clapham with the return North Yorkshireman from Skipton to Carnforth on 15 August 1979.

Above: On the evening of 7 September 1980 the Taysider, bound for Falkirk, is seen climbing near Kingskettle in Fife hauled by LNER D49 class 4–4–0 No 246 *Morayshire*.

Right: During the summer of 1980 British Railways ran a series of weekly specials between Manchester and Liverpool as part of the Rocket 150 celebrations. On 29 June 1980 LMS Pacific No 6201 *Princess Elizabeth* climbs away from St Helens Junction on the outward journey.

Previous page, Top left: LNER Class V2 2–6–2 No 4771 *Green Arrow* makes a splendid sight as it storms along near Copmanthorpe on the York circular route with the Centenary Express on 29 September 1979. This train which ran as part of the centenary of on-train catering was composed of historic railway dining vehicles and Pullman cars from the National Railway Museum at York.

Bottom left: On 2 June 1979, The Midlander, organised by SLOA, hurries through Craven Arms on the Shrewsbury–Hereford stage of its journey hauled by Class 5 4–6–0 No 5000.

Right: Merchant Navy Pacific No 35028 *Clan Line* threads the city walls of Chester with a train from Liverpool to Hereford on 21 June 1980. This train was billed as the Clan Line Farewell, the engine then remaining at Hereford for general repair and retubing.

Right: *Flying Scotsman* thunders through Clapham station with the Carnforth–Skipton portion of the Cumbrian Mountain Express on 1 March 1980.

Class A4 Pacific No 60009 *Union of South Africa* storms through Falkland Road, Fife, with a special bound for Edinburgh on 14 April 1979.

Nearing the summit of Lindal bank, Dalton, is Class A4
4–6–2 No 4498 *Sir Nigel Gresley* with the southbound
Cumbrian Coast Express on 23 August 1978.

Top left: During May 1976 long-preserved LNWR Precedent class 2–4–0 No 790 *Hardwicke* ran a series of specials between Carnforth and Grange-over-Sands. On 23 May *Hardwicke* is shown on the outward train between Silverdale and Arnside.

Left: On the Oxford–Worcester line, which no longer sees any steam activity, 4–6–0s No 7808 *Cookham Manor* and No 6998 *Burton Agnes Hall* are pictured near Drakes Broughton bound for Worcester and Hereford with a Great Western Society train on 14 June 1975.

Above: Burton Agnes Hall is seen again, this time near Cookham with a Bourne End to Maidenhead train. The occasion was the Marlow Donkey Centenary marking one hundred years of the Marlow branch on 15 July 1973.

Left: LNER Class D49 4–4–0 *Morayshire* climbs out of Dunfermline and approaches Townhill junction with the Falkirk–Dundee section of the Taysider special on 7 September 1980.

Above: On a very wet 14 August 1979, Jubilee class 4–6–0 No 5690 *Leander* makes a spirited start out of Carnforth with the northbound Cumbrian Coast Express.

Above: Veteran North British Railway Class J36 0–6–0 *Maude* crosses the Forth Bridge at North Queensferry with a southbound special to Edinburgh and Falkirk organised by the Scottish Railway Preservation Society on 4 May 1980. Note the painters' cradle slung beneath the bridge.

Top right: Thames launches and steam make a fascinating contrast as No 6998 *Burton Agnes Hall* crosses the Thames near Bourne End with a Bourne End–Maidenhead train as part of the Marlow branch centenary on 15 July 1973.

Right: *Sir Nigel Gresley* cautiously crosses Eskmeals viaduct south of Ravenglass with the return Cumbrian Coast Express. This was the first day of this service, 11 July 1978, and was organised by BR.

Left: Storming round a curve near Earlswood Lakes on the North Warwickshire line is V2 2–6–2 No 4771 *Green Arrow* with an LCGB special from Birmingham (Moor Street) to Stratford-on-Avon. 10 June 1973.

Above: On a bitterly cold 19 January 1980 GWR Castle class 4–6–0 No 5051 *Dryslwyn Castle* pounds up the bank out of Stratford-on-Avon with a Great Western Society special returning to Didcot.

Above: Jubilee 4–6–0 No 5596 *Bahamas* pauses at Grindleford before proceeding to Sheffield to take out a return special to Manchester via the Hope Valley route on 17 June 1973. This example of the preserved Jubilees is the only one to have a double chimney.

Right upper and lower: Flying Scotsman and *Lord Nelson* at Carnforth on Cumbrian Coast Express duty, 11 July 1978 and 1 July 1980 respectively.

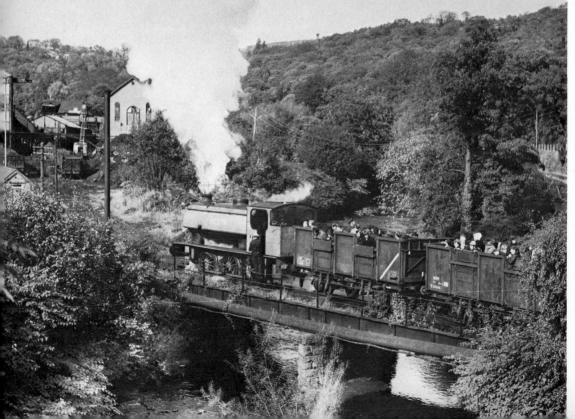

Three scenes showing the Monmouthshire Railway Society Deep Duffryn Diddler tour on 20 October 1979 from Newport which was steam-hauled over the NCB system at Mountain Ash by 0–6–0ST No 8. Although not strictly a BR steam special it is appropriate to include these photographs because of the close links between enthusiasts and industrial steam over the last few years and where better than the steam Mecca of Mountain Ash.

Top left: Crossing Afon Cynon to return to Mountain Ash station.

Left: Leaving the colliery yard for Aberaman.

Above: Pulling out of Mountain Ash station for the colliery.

Right: *Flying Scotsman* sets out from York with the Comet, bound for Manchester on 29 September 1979.

Next page, top left: What was a rare occurrence even in BR steam days, a WR Castle on the Lickey incline No 7029 *Clun Castle* climbs the 1 in 37 of Lickey with a special return working from Hereford to Tyseley on 8 October 1978.

Bottom left: Jubilee 4–6–0 No 5596 *Bahamas* is seen in the attractive setting of Grindleford with a Sheffield–Manchester special via the Hope Valley route on 17 June 1973.

Top right: Entering Hereford with a northbound train on 14 October 1972 is *King George V*. The journey on to Shrewsbury was completed by Jubilee 4–6–0 No 5596 *Bahamas*.

Bottom right: Pannier tank No 7752 struggles up the climb out of Woodend tunnel on the North Warwickshire line with a Stratford-on-Avon–Birmingham Moor Street special on 13 May 1973.

Above: The unusual combination of *King George V* and *Flying Scotsman*, one-time rivals and probably the best known engines in the world, ease into Hereford with the northbound Western Venturer on 22 September 1973.

Right: *Green Arrow* speeds through Earlswood Lakes station with a Birmingham–Stratford-on-Avon special on 10 June 1973.

Above: The southbound Taysider hauled by 4–4–0 *Morayshire* climbs through the rock cutting at North Queensferry on 7 September 1980.

Right: 4–6–0 *Lord Nelson* approaches Ulverston with the northbound Cumbrian Coast Express. 25 August 1980.

End of Steam. On 11 August 1968 the crowds gathered at
Ais Gill (*above*) to see Britannia Pacific No 70013 *Oliver
Cromwell* with the Fifteen Guinea Special, which apart
from the odd trip by 4472 was to be the last run by steam
on BR main lines until 2 October 1971 when *King George
V* (*top right*) drew crowds of people as it approached
Solihull bound for Birmingham from Hereford.

Right: Stanier Princess Pacific No 6201 speeds through
Dorrington, south of Shrewsbury with a Hereford train on
20 May 1978.

Above: LMS Class 5 4–6–0 No 5000 and Class 4 2–6–0 No 43106 make a splendid sight as they haul the Welsh Dragon up Llanvihangel bank towards Hereford on 11 October 1980.

Top Right: An unusual pairing on 26 May 1979 when Midland compound 4–4–0 No 1000 piloted LNER Class V2 2–6–2 *Green Arrow* with the Curator, bound for York, seen here climbing to Chinley.

Right: Double heading vintage stock at Laurieston on 3 August 1975 near the start of their journey from the SRPS depot at Falkirk to Darlington, via Edinburgh, for the Rail 150 celebrations later that month, are LNER 4–4–0 *Morayshire* and Caledonian 0–4–4 tank No 419.

Top left: 4472 crosses Garsdale viaduct bound for Appleby for the memorial service for the Rt Rev Eric Treacy on 30 September 1978.

Above: Garsdale viaduct, this time with LMS Class 5 4–6–0 No 5305 and the northbound Cumbrian Mountain Express on 1 March 1980.

Left: The same day saw 9F 2–10–0 *Evening Star* also bound for the service at Appleby. The location is between Horton and Ribblehead, a favourite photographic location of the late Bishop.

SR 4–6–0 *Lord Nelson* pulls out of Grange-over-Sands with the southbound Cumbrian Coast Express on 1 July 1980. This was the first run with a passenger train after restoration since its withdrawal by BR in 1962.

Above: LNER Class K1 2–6–0 No 2005 pulls out of Stockton with the Moorlander special between Middlesbrough and Newcastle on 22 October, 1978. The splendid station roof has, alas, since been demolished.

Next page: A sight that is now but a memory, for this beautiful set of GWR coaches from the GWS depot at Didcot is no longer allowed to run on BR metals. GWR 4–6–0s Nos 7808 and 5900 are seen near Kings Sutton on a lovely autumn morning bound for Hereford from Didcot via Birmingham on 6 October 1979.

Above: LMS Coronation Pacific No 46229 *Duchess of Hamilton* speeds round a curve near Pannal on the York circular train on 10 May 1980.

Right upper and lower: LNER 4472 *Flying Scotsman* and LMS Royal Scot 4–6–0 No 6115 *Scots Guardsman* are caught by the camera as they speed through Bolton Percy south of York, with northbound specials on 29 September 1979 and 14 October 1978 respectively.

Top left: LNER Class B1 4–6–0 No 1306 gets coaled up at Carnforth depot before leaving with a special on 10 August 1975.

Left: D49 4–4–0 *Morayshire* receives attention at Falkirk depot of the SRPS before leaving with 0–4–4 tank No 419 for Darlington and the Rail 150 celebrations on 3 August 1975.

Above: On the occasion of the start of the BR York circular trains on 25 June 1978, *Green Arrow* waits in York station before taking out the afternoon train. Note on this beautifully turned out engine the signal gantry reflected in the smoke box door.

Above: On a misty October evening, Royal Scot 4–6–0 No 6115 *Scots Guardsman*, thunders southbound out of York with the Anniversary Express bound for Manchester on 14 October 1978.

Top right: A4 Pacific No 60009 climbs up to the Forth Bridge with an Edinburgh to Aberdeen train on 14 April 1979.

Right: No 1000 and 4771 climb into Chinley with a York train on 26 May 1979..

Top left: An LNER pairing as B1 1305 and A3 4472 are caught by the evening sun as they cross Eskmeals viaduct, south of Ravenglass with a southbound special on 8 May 1976.

Above: Crossing the Severn at Worcester is *Burton Agnes Hall* with a GWS special from Didcot to Hereford on 24 June 1973.

Left: 5690 *Leander* climbs up to Clapham with a Carnforth train on 15 August 1979.

Above: Sadly for the British enthusiast GWR Castle 4–6–0 *Pendennis Castle* is now in Australia but on 6 April 1974 it was photographed near Dinmore on a Newport–Shrewsbury train.

Top right: Dart Valley Railway's GWR 0–4–2 tank No 1450 was borrowed to work the Marlow Donkey Centenary train, seen near Bourne End on 15 July 1973.

Right: Merchant Navy 4–6–2 No 35028 *Clan Line* climbs Hatton bank with a special train for Stratford-on-Avon on 26 October 1974.

York Departures
Above: A4 Pacific *Sir Nigel Gresley* departs with the
Merseyside Express neck and neck with a Doncaster
bound dmu on 29 September 1979.

Right: 9F 2–10–0 *Evening Star* heads the York circular on
9 July 1978.

Next page

Top left: *Clan Line* accelerates away from Stratford-on-Avon with a Didcot train on 26 October 1974.

Bottom left: Jubilee 4–6–0 No 5690 *Leander* at Chinley North Junction with the Leander Envoy special on 24 February 1979.

Top right: *Flying Scotsman* pulls out of Carnforth with the northbound Cumbrian Coast Express on 11 July 1978.

Bottom right: *Scots Guardsman* leaves Chinley with a York train on 10 November 1978.

Who would have thought of seeing a North British 0–6–0 on the Ais Gill route, but it happened on 17 May 1980 when *Maude* was photographed in splendid evening sunlight as it rounds a curve at Dent, bound for the Liverpool & Manchester 150th Anniversary celebrations at Rainhill.

Next page

Left: No 5690 *Leander* pulls out of Ravenglass and crosses the River Esk with the northbound Cumbrian Coast Express on 1 July 1980.

Top right: 2–4–0 *Hardwicke* crosses Eskmeals viaduct on a trial trip from Carnforth to Sellafield and return in preparation for the Rail 150 celebrations on 22 July 1975.

Bottom right: LMS Class 5 4–6–0 No 5000 leaves Newport for Hereford and crosses the River Usk with the Midlander railtour on 2 June 1979.

Top left: GWR large 2–6–2T 6106 climbs a rise near Cookham with a Maidenhead–Bourne End train on 15 July 1973.

Bottom left: LNWR 2–4–0 No 790 *Hardwicke* pulls out of Grange-over-Sands with an evening train to Carnforth on 23 May 1976.

Above: GWR 0–4–2 tank No 1450 near Marlow with the Marlow–Bourne End centenary train on 15 July 1973.

Top: Class 5 4–6–0 No 5000 climbs out of Hereford with the Newport section of the Midlander on 2 June 1979.

Above: David Shepherd's Class 9F 2–10–0 No 92203 *Black Prince* leaves Salisbury with an Eastleigh train on 20 April 1974.

Top right: LNER Class K1 2–6–0 No 2005 skirts the sea near Hartlepool with a Middlesbrough–Newcastle train on 22 October 1978.

Right: *Green Arrow* storms through Pannal with the first BR York circular train on 25 June 1978.

Top: Against the misty background of the Long Mynd *King George V* heads north for Shrewsbury with the Cydermaker special on 13 October 1979.

Above: *Hardwicke* climbs out of Millom with a special trial run to Sellafield on 22 July 1975.

Right: In foul weather LMS Class 5 No 5000 and Class 4 No 43106 climb towards Church Stretton with the Welsh Dragon railtour bound for Newport on 11 October 1980.

Above: Gresley Pacific No 60009 *Union of South Africa* rounds a curve near Wormit with an Edinburgh to Aberdeen railtour on 6 September 1980.

Top right: Class B1 4–6–0 No 1306 and A3 4–6–2 No 4472 *Flying Scotsman* are seen climbing north of Millom with a Sellafield train on 8 May 1976.

Right: *Evening Star*, the last steam locomotive built for BR, hurries through Micklefield with a York circular train on 9 July 1978.

Left: The southbound Deeside Venturer hauled by *King George V* speeds over the Dee viaduct at Pentre on 4 October 1980.

Above: On 11 November 1980 LMS Pacific No 46229 *Duchess of Hamilton* climbs through the suburbs of Leeds bound for York via Church Fenton. This train which started at Liverpool and ran to Leeds via Manchester and the Standedge route was operated to commemorate the 150th anniversary of Mail by Rail.

Left: Far from home Southern Merchant Navy Pacific *Clan Line* climbs to Birkett Tunnel with one of the return workings from the memorial service for Bishop Eric Treacy at Appleby on 30 September 1978.

Above: LNER A4 4–6–2 No 4498 *Sir Nigel Gresley* crosses Long Marton viaduct near Appleby with a southbound special on 22 October 1978.

Glowing in the winter sunshine GW Castle class 4–6–0 No 5051 *Drysllwyn Castle* climbs out of Stratford-on-Avon bound for Didcot with the GWS train on 26 January 1980. This was the last time that these GWR coaches were allowed to run on BR.

City Departures (*next page*)
Right: North British 0–6–0 *Maude* passes Haymarket station Edinburgh with a special to Falkirk on 4 May 1980.

Left: 5690 *Leander* winds its way out of Manchester near Liverpool Road Junction with the BR Manchester–Liverpool train on 9 July 1980.

Above: The Cydermaker hauled by *King George V* bound for Hereford climbs up Baystone Hill out of Shrewsbury on a very wet 13 October 1979.

Top right: LMS 4–6–0 No 6115 *Scots Guardsman* leaves Chinley with a Sheffield–Manchester special on 21 September 1978.

Right: The northbound Midlander pulls out of Hereford with LMS Class 5 4–6–0 No 5000 in charge on 2 June 1979.

Above and right: Two night studies of *Sir Nigel Gresley* at
Carnforth after working in with the Santa Steam Special
on 29 December 1979.